Old Plaistow. A paper read at the Balaam
Street Schools, Plaistow ... Illustrated by
Spedding Curwen. With an appendix by the
Rev. R. W. B. Marsh. [With illustrations.]

John Spencer Curwen, Spedding Curwen

July 2014

To Len

Wishing you the very best of every-
thing - today and always.

Love and very best wishes
    Marion & George   xx

    Congratulations!
For the 9th July 1934

Old Plaistow. A paper read at the Balaam Street Schools, Plaistow ... Illustrated by Spedding Curwen. With an appendix by the Rev. R. W. B. Marsh. [With illustrations.]

Curwen, John Spencer
British Library, Historical Print Editions
British Library
Curwen, Spedding
1892
60 p. ; 8°.
10350.de.30.

The BiblioLife Network

GUIDE TO FOLD-OUTS, MAPS and OVERSIZED IMAGES

LD

ASTOW

SECOND EDITION

OLD PLAISTOW.

Wrought Iron Gate of Essex Lodge

ESSEX

LODGE

FRONTISPIECE (see p. 6).

SECOND EDITION.

OLD PLAISTOW

A PAPER READ AT THE BALAAM STREET SCHOOLS,
PLAISTOW, OCTOBER 15TH, 1891,

BY

JOHN SPENCER CURWEN.

ILLUSTRATED BY

SPEDDING CURWEN.

WITH AN APPENDIX BY THE

REV. R. W. B. MARSH, M.A.

"THEY'RE DUCK'S, SIR!" (see p. 41.)

*All the proceeds of the sale of this book will be devoted to the Plaistow
Sick Poor Society, founded 1841.*

Plaistow:
H. PARKER, 198, BALAAM STREET.
1892

PREFACE.

THE hearty reception of this paper afforded a most gratifying proof of the affection and pride still felt for " Old Plaistow " by those who live there. One would have thought that the hand of the builder and " developer " had weakened such interest. But men and women happily change less than their surroundings. Old landmarks may be removed, but memories and traditions are more durable.

In reprinting the paper I have inserted one or two paragraphs that want of time forced me to omit during delivery, while conversations with the Rev. R. W. B. Marsh and Mr. Henry Hay and others have enabled me here and there to amplify information or to correct small details. Mr. Marsh's valuable recollections appear in an Appendix. The interest of the narrative is greatly enhanced by the sketches of old Plaistow houses which my brother, Mr. Spedding Curwen, J.P., has contributed. All the sketches, except a few otherwise acknowledged, are from his hand.

It is sad to think that, between the delivery of this lecture and its publication, two of my most valued informants—the Rev. Thomas Perfect and Dr. William Marten Cooke — have passed away.

It is scarcely necessary to add that this essay is intended for Plaistow people. To others, many of the details will appear trivial. What Mr. Thomas Hardy calls " the earth love " makes all the difference.

J. S. C.

OLD PLAISTOW.

SUNDAY School teacher was once telling a scholar of all the beauties and charms of the Garden of Eden. The girl listened attentively, but when the teacher had finished, she said, "That's all very well; but what you have been telling me happened a long time ago. I expect that place you've been talking about is all built over now." I should say, from internal evidence, that that girl came from Plaistow. "It is all built over now." That is how we have to end many a story of old Plaistow. And some people think that because of this Plaistow has lost its interest. Nothing of the sort. We have exchanged a country village for a town, a small group of people for a crowd; but the story and romance still linger about the old streets. It is just a question how much knowledge and imagination you can put into the discovery of them. I myself cannot put much of either, and only offer you a few rambling remarks. But even if Plaistow were less interesting than it is it would be our duty to discuss its past. Here many of us were born, and more have lived; we are drawn to the place by a hundred ties, and it is the business of every one to stand up for the place to which he belongs. It is patriotism on a small scale. For me the past has always possessed a fascination. The man who goes along with his eyes on the ground becomes narrow. Whereas if you cultivate habits of observation and reflection you will find that what seems the dullest of places becomes intellectually stimulating. In putting together these remarks, I have received much kind help from such old inhabitants as Rev. Thomas Perfect, Mr. Cohu, Mr. and Miss Perry, Mr. and Mrs. McDowall, Mrs. Lawn, Mr. and Miss Seale, Mr. Graves, Mr. Boddy, Mr. Hollamby, Mr. Mills, jun., and Rev. R. W. B. Marsh. I have also re-read Miss Fry's "History," which was

B

so carefully edited by Dr. Pagenstecher. Please understand that although I may not always mention their names, I am constantly indebted to these friends for my facts. I cannot honestly say that my own memory goes back more than thirty-eight years, but I have always been in the habit of talking with older men and women on this subject.

Where shall I begin? A word first as to the formation of the ground we stand on. Geologists say that the Thames valley, in which we are, is formed by a depression, through which a river has found its way. We will start with the chalk, which underlies the whole county, and is the bottom of an old ocean. Here it is some way down, but it peeps out at Purfleet and Grays. The other strata you may have seen if you looked down the trench when the new drainage works were lately made. Lowest of all, the blue London clay, hard and stiff, originally laid down in the sea beyond the mouth of a large estuary. Above it in some places light-coloured sand, another evidence of the sea. Then gravel, a river deposit, and at the top rich loam. As you near the marsh the gravel decreases and the loam increases. Many of you saw the excavations for the Victoria, or at least for the Albert Dock, before the water was let in. They laid bare the story of the river drift on which the Canning Town district is built. Large trees of various kinds were encountered as the digging proceeded. The wood was hardened and black, but well preserved. Even the small branches, containing sometimes acorns and nuts, came to light. These trees had been washed down from the upper parts of the Thames valley in time of flood before the river wall was made. The sediment of the river had soon covered them, and there they lay for thousands of years until the new dock was made.

The name of "Plaistow" is generally derived from Hugh de Plaiz, once the Lord of the Manor. It is the stow or village of de Plaiz. But the Rev. Dr. Smyth Palmer, vicar of Holy Trinity, Wanstead, who is a leading authority on the names of places, writes to me in answer to my enquiry:—"'Plaistow,' as you know, means the 'play place,' and it is found in Aelfric's Anglo-Saxon Glossary (Cott. MSS. 95) in the form 'plegstow,' and with the explanation 'theatrum' (Ettmüller, Lexicon Anglo-Saxonicum, p. 275). The word seems to have been more generally used for a village green or play-ground. You will find a note on the Hants 'Pleystow' (or 'Plestor') in Gilbert White's 'Antiquities of Selborne,' Letter X. It is mentioned as 'La Pleystow' in 1271."

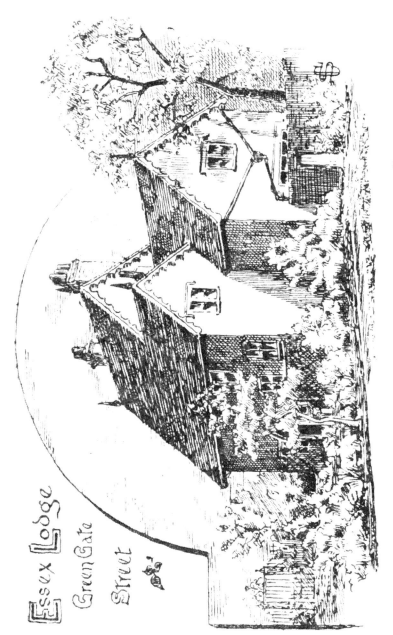

From a Photograph kindly lent by G. C. Mackrow, Esq.

Old Plaistow consists of five streets—Greengate Street, Balaam Street, North Street, Richmond Street, and High Street. These, at least, are the present names; but it is said that what we now call High, Richmond, and North Streets, originally had but one name—Cordwainer Street. Cordwainer means a worker in leather, and there may have been, at some remote time, a village industry of bootmaking established here. Balaam Street was formerly known as Balaam Lane. The name is peculiar, but as Balaam is a surname—I had a letter the other day from a Mr. Balaam—it may have come from an inhabitant or property owner. Greengate Street led to the green gate of the marshes—a gate, not to prevent people from going in, but to prevent cattle from straying off. The other means of keeping the cattle apart was by ditches, which were more formidable than fences, and required less repair. One of the early memories of my childhood are the marshmen, who went about with long jumping-poles on their shoulders. These poles had a flat circular base at one end. The marshmen placed this in the middle of the ditch and vaulted over easily. How did there come to be a village here so early, if we follow Miss Fry, as the sixteenth century? I have no doubt it was the rich pastures of the river marshes that caused the settlement. Plaistow lies on the edge of what was then the firm ground —as near to the marsh as could be. The villagers would be chiefly occupied in fattening cattle and rearing horses, and as a love of roast beef and of horses has existed in England for a good many centuries, so the early settlement of Plaistow is explained. But, though the marshes stretched to the south, there were on all other sides good land for corn and food stuffs and hay, and farming in all its branches flourished greatly. Incidentally I may mention that Plaistow, so far as the soil goes, must be a far more healthy place than it was centuries ago. The ground is drained, the old ponds are dried up, and the subsoil of gravel makes the damp disappear quickly. As to the marsh, it is infinitely more healthy for drainage. When the water was taken out of the marsh loam by drainage it shrunk like a sponge. I am told that a public-house in the Victoria Dock Road sank three feet. I suppose some teetotalers would have been glad if it had disappeared altogether. The church of St. John, North Woolwich, was built on piles, and after a time the piles came up through the floor and had to be sawn off, or rather, properly speaking, the church sank down. But this process is now pretty well over. Any present danger to health does not rise from the ground, but floats in the air—the artificial pollution caused by factories. But as I understand that the whole prosperity of the district is due to the fact that here any manufacturer can make what smoke and smell he pleases, I suppose I must not complain.

Old Houses & Pinnock's Place.

The old Plaistow houses are of various periods. There is the brick house tiled, the wooden house, the house made of timber filled in with lath and plaster, and there is one specimen of the old overhanging first storey. This is in Pinnock's Place, opposite St. Mary's Church, and adjoining the end of Smith's timber yard. I should say this is the oldest house now standing in Plaistow. There is a tradition that Admiral Benbow once lived there, but I have not been able to verify it. No doubt the house formerly stood by itself.

Let us take a start from this old house, and make a tour round the village, as it was in days long past. Where St. Mary's schools now are stood a horse-pond, which sometimes overflowed the road so that the Quakers, coming to meeting, had to walk on planks. St. Mary's Road was then known as Palsy Lane, and was full of wild flowers. On the old maps it is called Purls Hills Lane, of which name Palsy was probably a corruption. The corner house, where St. Mary's Road joins North Street, is now called Church House, but its old name was Pond House. Here the great grandfather of Mr. and Miss Seale came to live in the latter part of the last century, and there he died. On the right hand, passing up North Street, lived old Mrs. Billingay, who kept her money under a loose board on her parlour floor, and nearly lost it. Passing down Greengate Street, there were on the left-hand side a lot of cottages, occupied by Irish labourers. These labourers were brought over by Farmer James Adams to cultivate potatoes. They formed a colony by themselves, and I am told that the first generation of them was better than the subsequent ones have been. On the right hand side you may still see the old boundary wall of Essex House. There are traditions of this house going back three centuries and a half. It is said to have been the mansion of the Duke of Somerset, who was appointed Protector during the minority of Edward VI. Afterwards it was the residence of the Earl of Essex, who was beheaded by Queen Elizabeth. Later on it was successively a school and a mad-house. Mr. Charles Curtis pulled it down in 1836, and built Essex Lodge out of some of its materials. The earl's coronet is still on the old iron gate. The old house contained sixty rooms, with a spacious hall. I am sorry that I can find no mention of this property in Devereux's "Lives of the Earls of Essex." Further on is the "Greengate" public-house. There are five old inns in Plaistow—the "Greengate," the "Black Lion," the "Coach and Horses," the "Greyhound," and the "Abbey Arms." Of these, either the "Greengate" or the "Black Lion" is the oldest license; but the "Greengate," as it stands, built partly of wood, is the older house. The "Greengate Inn" gave upon the marshes, and was the end of civilization. Prince Regent Lane led from it to a public-house of that name which stood on the river side close to where the entrance to the Victoria Docks now is. The inn, and perhaps the lane, was probably so called from having been constructed during the Regency (1788-1820). The only other building on the Essex

Carved Stone Mantlepiece from Essex House, now erected in the Kitchen of Essex Lodge, bearing a Coronet and Crest.

shore was the barge house at North Woolwich. Return to the
Broadway. Here, on the south side, stood the biggest house
in Plaistow—Broadway House—residence for more than one
generation for the Marten family, well remembered for their good
deeds. Mr. Robert Humphrey Marten bought this house in 1806,
and resided in it until his death in December, 1839. Then his son,
Mr. Charles Marten, enlarged and improved it, and he and his
family lived there until his death in June, 1851. The family
removed to Blackheath in the autumn of that year, but did not sell
the property till 1867. It was pulled down some nine or ten years
ago. Dr. William Marten Cooke, a grandson of Robert Humphrey
Marten, is still able, at the age of 80, to recall his impressions of
the old house. "Here," he writes to me, "I once saw Mr.
Wilberforce, who was not an infrequent visitor, and who on this
occasion came down on the Saturday for Sunday, and worshipped
in the little chapel in North Street. This visit impressed itself the
more on my memory because the season had been a very hot
and dry one, and I was asked to assist the gardener in watering the
lawn (in which my grandfather took much pride) in preparation for
the visit." The space bounded by the Broadway, High, Richmond,
and North Streets was called in old days "the island," and
"walking round the island" was a familiar term.

I remember Mr. William Thodey, now in Australia (whose family
came to Plaistow in the last century), telling me that there was
once bull-baiting in the Broadway. The sport was so universal in
days gone by that it is certain to have been practised somewhere in
Plaistow, and the Broadway—called on old maps "Plaistow Cross"
—would be the most central spot. The bull was pinned to an iron
ring, and bulldogs were set upon him. On the north side of
the Broadway there were two or three houses, but the fields behind
them were open, and there were elm trees and a rookery. One
of these houses was occupied for a time by a Mr. Hall, who fired a
gun off in his back garden at ten o'clock every night, either to tell
his neighbours that it was time to retire, or to convey a hint
to possible burglars that he was ready for them. Come now to
High Street, and stand with your back to West Ham and your
face towards the marsh. Mary Simmonds, called "the Plaistow
giantess," lived in a cottage in High Street, opposite the entrance
to Victoria Road. There was a memoir of her in the *Family
Herald* many years since. Notice the ancient and massive brick
wall on the right hand side near the nursery. It is worked

Broadway
House &
Pulled down
1882.

The Residence of the Martin Family.

in bricks of two colours, and is evidently very old. This is one of the walls surrounding Hyde House, which stood opposite the "Black Lion," and which dates back at least to 1605. It was pulled down at the beginning of the century. Opposite this, just at the entrance to Church Street, stood, until 1839, Porch House, for many years a seat of the Rawstone family. The title deeds say that in the reign of Henry VIII it was considered the oldest house

Porch House
Cordwainers Lane
(Now High Street)
Pulled down
1839.

From an Old Painting by the late W. M. Haigh, kindly lent by Miss McPherson.

in Plaistow. It was pulled down in 1839, having been condemned by the surveyor. Mr. Curtis, of Stratford, the builder who pulled it down, said it would have stood for many more years. The house contained 26 rooms some 30 feet in length. The rafters supporting the roof were chestnut trees with the bark on, bolted together with iron bolts. The late Mr. W. M. Haigh, nurseryman, whom many old inhabitants will remember, was apprenticed to his uncle, Mr. McPherson, also a nurseryman, who rented the ground both before and after the old house was pulled down. Mr. Haigh slept in a bedroom which had a crack in the wall, through which the ivy grew and hung down inside, being almost colourless for want of light. Before Porch House disappeared, Mr. Haigh made an oil colour painting of it, which is still in the possession of Miss

McPherson. Mrs. Sanders, daughter of Mr. Haigh, has very kindly obtained the loan of the picture, and has supplied much of the foregoing information about the old house. The gardens and a carriage drive belonging to the house opened not only into High Street, but into Upton Lane, but Mr. McPherson, who wanted the land, ploughed up the drive, and removed the piers and stone balls from the gateway. A house nearly opposite, pulled down about the same time, is said to have been the residence of the Beauclerks.

Opposite Mr. Potter's shop, and behind what is now the Plaistow Postman's Office, there was, up till 1859, an old barn, which had a red brick arch for gateway, the date 1579, and the words, "This is the gate to everlasting life," cut in the brickwork. Many of us here remember it. The first twenty yards of the lane which led to it still remains as a piece of no-man's-land between the Wesleyan Church and Mrs. Shrimpton's crockery shop. The tradition is that when the monasteries were dissolved by Henry VIII, the monks of West Ham Abbey found refuge in this barn. The date seems rather late for this, as the second Act for dissolving the monasteries was passed forty years earlier; but I know no other explanation. When the great sewer was made, in 1859, this land was bought by the Metropolitan Board of Works, for they needed the gravel it contained for concrete, and the barn was pulled down. Several old inhabitants have told me that the inscription was taken to the offices of the Board in Spring Gardens, to be preserved as a curiosity. I have, however, made careful inquiries there, and have seen two of the staff who were there in 1859. They assure me that the inscription never reached the place. I fear that this interesting relic of old Plaistow was broken up at the time. Being of brick it would not be easily transported. The barn belonged to a farm house, which stood a few yards back from the road, nearly opposite Mr. Potter's, and was demolished at the same date. Mrs. Lawn, who, at an advanced, age, possesses a perfectly clear memory, tells me that her father, who was bailiff of the Manor, lived and died here. In one of the rooms were two large pictures, painted on the wooden panels in the wall. One represented the visit of the Queen of Sheba to Solomon, and the other Abraham and Isaac.

Further down, at the entrance to Balaam Street, just by the " Coach and Horses," Mr. Jackson has just built himself a new house. This displaced two old houses, which you must nearly all remember. These two houses were originally one, and in this house lived for a time the notorious Dr. Dodd. The son of a clergyman, he was ordained deacon and curate of West Ham in 1751, and soon after got the lectureship, which he resigned in 1766. While here he took pupils, one of whom was the Hon. Philip Stanhope, nephew of the Lord Chesterfield whose " letters to his son " are so well known. When he left West Ham, Dodd went to London, and started a chapel in Pimlico as a private

Dr. Dodd's house, which was pulled down in 1890, is drawn from a Photograph kindly lent by Mr. J. Jackson.

venture. A thorough ladies' man and a most unctuous preacher, he had a great following, and managed in a clever way to jumble up piety and dissipation. Later on he got into difficulties, and in 1777 (11 years after leaving West Ham) he offered a bond for £4,200 in the name of Lord Chesterfield to a stockbroker. This was his former pupil, who had meanwhile succeeded to the title. The signature was found to be a forgery. Dodd, being arrested, promptly returned £3,000, and Lord Chesterfield wanted the charge hushed up, but the Lord Mayor insisted upon going on with it. Extraordinary interest was manifested in the trial,

Dr. Johnson befriended Dr. Dodd. When he was condemned to death 23,000 people signed a petition for clemency; but it did not avail, and the whilom fashionable preacher was executed. Those who want to know more of Dr. Dodd without the trouble of referring to contemporary documents, will find his story told in Mr. Percy Fitzgerald's book, "A Famous Forgery." My judgment

About to be pulled down; said to have been the residence of Benjamin West.

of the doctor is founded on a careful perusal of his works. The forgery was not his only transgression. There is no doubt, however, that before death he became sincerely penitent. Close to Dr. Dodd's house (where Mr. Caines' office now is) stood a blacksmith's forge, and behind it an old house belonging the family of Swete, whose name is preserved in Swete Street. A few paces further, still on the right hand side of Balaam Street, stands an old house which is said to have been once the residence of Benjamin West, the celebrated painter of historical events. The summer house, still standing at the back, is his reputed studio. I have not been able to verify this tradition. West's "Life," though issued after his death, is virtually an autobiography, and though it mentions other places where he lived, I find nothing about Plaistow. I merely give the tradition as it has reached me.

Said to have been the Studio of Benjamin West.
Sketched from the garden by kind permission of Mrs. Gibbs.

In Chesterton House, now occupied by Dr. Kennedy, there lived, some fifty years ago, Luke Howard, F.R.S., founder of the chemical business at Stratford, now carried on by his descendants. Luke Howard died in 1864, but he left Plaistow long before. His name remains in Howard's Road. Luke Howard was a Quaker, and he bequeathed to Plaistow the valuable legacy of a pump. When he did so there were but few wells, and the cottagers must have been badly off for water. There was one other well at the "Abbey Arms," and one down Palsy Lane. Who does not remember Howard's pump —for so it was called to the end of its days—a few years ago? It stood in Chesterton Road, a few yards out of Balaam Street. At first it adjoined the house—the well is in the stable yard—but we all remember it on the right hand side, close to a cottage. The well, I believe, is a very deep one. On the other side of the road stands Plaistow Hall, for many years the residence of Mr. Charles Curtis, and more recently of his daughter, Mrs. Overbury. This is an old brick mansion which has been largely added to by successive occupiers. In the garden is a mulberry-tree, one of the finest and oldest in the village, which tradition says was planted by Henry VIII. Further down, on the right hand side beyond the dispensary, stands Brunstock Cottage, part of an old house with a weeping ash in front of it. Here, for a time (1759 to 1761) lived Edmund Burke, writer, orator, and politician. Sir James Prior, in his "Life of Burke," refers to the fact. "About this time," he says (1759), "Mr. Burke occasionally resided at Plaistow, in Essex. A lady, then about 14 years old, and residing in that neighbourhood, informs the writer that she perfectly remembers him there; that his brother Richard lived chiefly with him, and that they were much noticed in the neighbourhood for talents and sociable qualities, and particularly for having a variety of visitors, who were understood to be authors soliciting a private opinion of their works, and not infrequently men of rank." Burke left Plaistow for Dublin in 1761. He had been married two years when he came here, and was closely occupied in literary work and political wire-pulling. "Even to late in life," says Sir James Prior, "he delighted in children—his 'men in miniature,' spinning tops or teetotums with his boy visitors— turning from time to time to older guests to throw out some forcible truth in human nature from the scene which their habits, passions, and contentions afforded." There is a pleasant picture to associate with the old house. The story, that while here Burke wrote his essay on "The Sublime and the Beautiful" will not hold water. It is clear from his life that this could not have been so.

At the point where the sewer crosses Balaam Street, there were on the left hand side some old houses, in one of which the Piegrome family carried on for 120 years the occupation of shoemakers; and as Mr. Graves was apprenticed to Mr. Piegrome, and has himself carried on the trade in Plaistow for 60 years, he is certainly in the apostolic succession as regards shoemaking. When Miss Fry wrote

her history, the Piegromes were still living in their house, and they
possessed a pattern for a pair of buckled shoes marked " Honble.
Philip Stanhope." They had been employed to make them for Dr.
Dodd's pupil, whose signature he afterwards forged.

At the bottom of Balaam Street, on the right hand side, was a
house occupied by Mr. Warmington, who is still commemorated by
a street hard by. This was a good house, and had a park round it.

Pulled down in 1882.   From a Photograph kindly lent by Mr. Thos. Cohu.

The grounds stretched from Whitwell Road to Barking Road. At
the foot was a ditch, in which water-lilies grew. Mr. Kelland
occupied the house subsequently to Mr. Warmington, and his name
is preserved in Kelland Road. Beyond stands the " Abbey Arms,"
the modern successor of an older inn.

Cross the Barking Road, go straight on, turn to the left, and you
are at Cumberland House, named after Henry, Duke of Cumberland, brother of George III, who kept his racing stud here. He
was a young man who died in 1790 at the age of 24. Mrs. Skelton,
wife of his head groom, kept house, and he would often pass the
night there, attended by only one servant. The old house is

entirely unaltered. The kitchen, with its great high fireplace,
massive dressers and wainscoated walls, speaks of old days. The
hall and staircase are solidly built, and some of the rooms have
double doors. In the farmyard stands an ancient barn, said to be
the largest in Essex, and perhaps the most interesting relic left in
Plaistow at the present time. Pacing it roughly, I should say

Old Barn & Cumberland House

it stands on the ground 120 feet
by 40. The tiled roof comes down
low, and the height is very great.
Standing inside, you see a forest
of great beams, and smaller ones all morticed in. These beams,
it is said, are of horse chestnut wood, which the wire worm will
not touch. This barn carries us back much earlier than Cumberland House. It probably belonged to the Abbey of West Ham in
the 15th or 16th century, and was used for tenants to assemble on
rent and tithe days. In the loft there are traces of partitions and
plaster; evidently farm hands have slept there. The timbers have
now a decided slope, but the immense strength of the structure,
which has supported the barn for at least 300 years, will serve it for
some time yet. The property now belongs to the Coopers'
Company.

Corner of the Barn at
Cumberland House

Showing about half the length of the Interior of the Barn.
Sketched by kind permission of the present occupier, Mr. Mills.

I have said nothing about the Barking Road. That is a modern work; this is evident from its straightness. When the East India Docks were made, at the beginning of the century, the old ferry from Poplar gave way to the Iron Bridge, and a road was made to Barking. Before that, the access to Barking had been long; the coach had to go through Stratford and Ilford. Old inhabitants still call this the "new road," though it was made 1807-10. The making of it was a sanguine effort; for years it was scarcely used. Up to thirty or forty years ago there were only six houses between the "Abbey Arms" and the Iron Bridge. One of these was the "Half-way House Inn;" there was also a marshman's cottage, and, strangest of all, a ladies' boarding-school. How deserted the road was at this time you may realise by the fact that a lady still living at Plaistow dropped her watch on the path just this side of the Iron Bridge, reached home before she discovered her loss, and went back and found the watch untouched. Mr. Henry Hay tells me that he has often walked from the "Abbey Arms" to the gates of the East India Dock without seeing a soul except the tollman on the Iron Bridge, who for years did not take enough to pay his wages. The new road, being run through the marsh, had a poor foundation, and was at first very rotten. The driver of the Barking coach, which ran over the Iron Bridge, had to run his vehicle along the path, for which he was duly summoned and fined. Along the sides of the road were ditches with willows growing in them, where the white satin moth hovered, and the reed-warbler built its bottle-shaped nest. At the Iron Bridge end was a reed bed, which I remember yielded us boys excellent arrows. The marsh itself was in winter the haunt of swarms of wild fowl, and as the shooting was practically free, and nearly every working man had a gun, there was plenty of sport. Herons fished in the ditches, and an east wind brought thousands of plover, duck, teal, widgeon, and snipe. The best way was to go out by night, lie low, and wait for the dawn. It was cold work, but I am told it was capital sport. I can testify too that the ditches were fine places for skating. You could go, as in Holland, straight on for miles.

The village of Plaistow was entirely rural. You may find such villages now between here and Chelmsford. People still living remember that oxen were used, not only for ploughing, but for drawing waggons along the streets. Great elms, planted two hundred years before, lined the streets. The cottages were hemmed in with banks of sweet briar. In the gardens were lilac, laburnum, and wallflowers; the place was leafy, bowery, bright, and scented.

The only street I have left unnoticed is Richmond Street. Here stands Richmond House, which I know well, because I spent my boyhood there. It was formerly occupied by Mr. Bosanquet, one of the vicars of St. Mary's, who bought it from the Duke of Richmond. He was known as "mad Bosanquet," only, I fancy, because he was a little unclerical in his ways, liberal-minded, and energetic. The son of the banker of that name, he had money at command. A bachelor when he came to Plaistow, he would have four or five poor families living with him in Richmond House, and would take some of them up to town to dine at his father's. "I happened to be at Plaistow," writes Dr. W. M. Cooke to me, "when Mr. Bosanquet made his first appearance, and startled the people of the quiet village by the energy of his move-ments, which led some to doubt whether he was quite sane. The first report I heard of him was that he had called on a poor woman, one of the chapel people, who was boiling down a bullock's head, and whom he shocked by the exclamation, 'What the devil have you got there?'" Mr. Bosanquet held the land opposite the house, and began to bore a tunnel under the road, so as to connect his two properties; but the authorities stopped the tunnel. He rode a white pony, and used to make the boys of St. Mary's school rub it down. In a book dated 1840, he speaks of Plaistow as an agricultural village. Richmond House was a good specimen of old-fashioned 18th century houses, of which there were formerly so many in Plaistow. The ground floor had wainscoted walls; in the kitchen fireplaces were quaint porcelain tiles representing Scripture incidents. The garden, now covered with Jeyes' factory, yielded mulberries, apples, pears, quinces, walnuts, and bush fruit in great abundance.

Not properly in Plaistow, but standing half-a-mile away, in Green Street, is "Anne Boleyn's Tower," or "Green Street House," called also in my youth "Morley's Castle," from the name of the then owner. I wrote a full account of this house in the *Stratford Express*, Oct. 9th, 1869. Two antiquarians, who visited it in 1824, and recorded their impressions in the *Gentleman's Magazine*, con-sidered the tower to be at least 300 years old. They were received on their visit by the proprietor, Mr. Morley, an active of old gentleman of more than eighty, who told them he had drunk nothing but water for forty years, and maintained the then novel doctrine that strong liquors prematurely exhaust the energies of body and mind. He had lived at the place (in 1824) for fifty years, and told his visitors of the tradition which associates the house and tower with Anne Boleyn and Henry VIII. Henry, said he, built the tower for the amusement of his betrothed, for it gave her a fine view of the Thames. The room in the third storey was formerly hung with leather, richly decorated with gold, and

Copy of a Water Colour Painting by Miss Katherine Fry,
sketched in 1868 for G. E. Linnington, Esq.

Mr. Morley's predecessor burnt it for the sake of the gold, which he sold for £30. Mr. Morley cultivated mistletoe on his grounds, by pressing the berries against a tree at Christmas time. The berry adhered by its viscous juice, and became a plant. When the house was bought as a Reformatory School for Roman Catholic boys about 1868, the old ivy-crowned archway disappeared. When writing about this house in 1869, I asked Mr. J. A. Froude if he had ever heard of the place. He replied : " I never met with any letter of Henry VIII dated from Green-street, nor did I ever meet with the name in connection with him, or with Anne Boleyn, or afterwards, that I can recollect, with Elizabeth." Still there must be some foundation for the local tradition. Many will remember the Morley family, who held the house until about 1867 or 1868.

On the back of the sketch from which our illustration is taken, Miss Fry wrote :—"Green-street House, in the parish of East Ham ; drawn from a rural lane known as Pursey Lane (now Tilbury Road). It is now known as 'Boleyn Castle,' or 'Boleyn Tower,' from a tradition that it was a hunting-seat of King Henry VIII, and that he built the tower for Anna Boleyn to see the shipping on the river ; also that when his jealousy was first excited at the Tournament at Greenwich, she was shut up in this tower until her removal to the Tower of London."

About the middle of last century, Dick Turpin, the highwayman, was the terror of this district. Son of an innkeeper at Hempstead, near Saffron Walden, he was apprenticed to a butcher in White-chapel, got dismissed for his bad behaviour, came as servant to Farmer Giles, at a house in Richmond Street, went from bad to worse, and began his lawless career by stealing two of Farmer Giles's fat oxen. These he took home and cut up. The skins, sold at Waltham Abbey, were recognised, a warrant was issued, and Turpin only evaded arrest by leaping out of a window when the officers came. Henceforth he was at war with society for something like ten years. He led a gang of smugglers in the district between here and Southend ; not only did he smuggle, but he would stop other smugglers in the King's name, and make them deliver up their spoils. Next he settled in Epping Forest with a few choice friends, and stole deer from the parks around. Later he took to housebreaking. His party would surprise a house by day, bind the inmates, and get the money. At one house he sat an old woman on the fire till she would tell where her money was. Once he and his gang were surprised in an ale-house in Westminster, and all were taken but Turpin, who again leaped from the window. After this he went into partnership with a man named King. They dug a cave in a thicket between Loughton Road and King's Oak Road, and kept it covered with green branches. It was large enough to conceal and shelter the two men and their horses, while they could watch the people passing on either road. Turpin had married a wife, Hester Palmer, from East Ham, and she was faithful to him, going to market and supplying him with food, some-times staying a week at a time in the cave. It seems incredible that the highwaymen lived here for six years ; but the Forest was at that time little frequented. The collection of pistols, swords, spurs, &c., found in the forest, which is now at the "Wake Arms," forms visible evidence of the rough play that went on there in those times. Meanwhile the reward for Turpin's arrest, offered by the Government, started at £50 and got up to £200. One day Turpin, returning from a raid, found his horse tired. He saw a gentleman riding in front on a thoroughbred, and in his usual way put his pistol to the gentleman's head, and suggested that they should exchange mounts. When the gentleman got home, he learned that 'the horse he was riding had been stolen from the Plaistow Marshes, and the saddle from someone else. A day or two later the thoroughbred was stabled in a London inn, and the landlord, getting wind of the story, tried to arrest Turpin. There was a scuffle, and Turpin, by accident, shot his friend King instead of the landlord. He got off, but was heart-broken. Then the Loughton thicket became too hot for him. They hunted him with bloodhounds, and he saw the dogs pass under the tree into which he had climbed. Off he went to Yorkshire, took the name of Palmer, and for a time did legitimate business as a horse dealer. But one day, out of sheer mischief, he shot a game cock; the owner put him in prison; inquiries were made about him, and it was found that some of the horses he had sold were not his own. Then Turpin did a rash thing. He wrote to his brother at Hempstead, the brother would not pay the postage, and the village schoolmaster happened to see the letter at the post-office, and recognised Turpin's writing. Thus it was that the Yorkshire people found that their prisoner Palmer was the great Turpin. He was tried for horsestealing at the York Assizes, and executed April 7th, 1739, when only in his 33rd year. He told the judge that he expected to be tried in Essex, and begged them to send him back to his native county, where, he said, plenty of people would speak for him. I fear that this was only an excuse. Turpin was a popular hero. A contemporary writer says that all along he was more admired than blamed; and this we can understand, for he possessed just those qualities of daring, endurance, and resource, on which we English set such high value. There was also a touch of generosity mingled with his deeds of violence. Once he robbed a widow, but hearing afterwards that her landlord was pressing her for rent, he rode by her door, and without drawing rein, tossed some guineas on to the floor. Again, he stopped a man, who said with tears, that he had only eighteen-pence upon him. Turpin gave him half-a-crown and rode on.

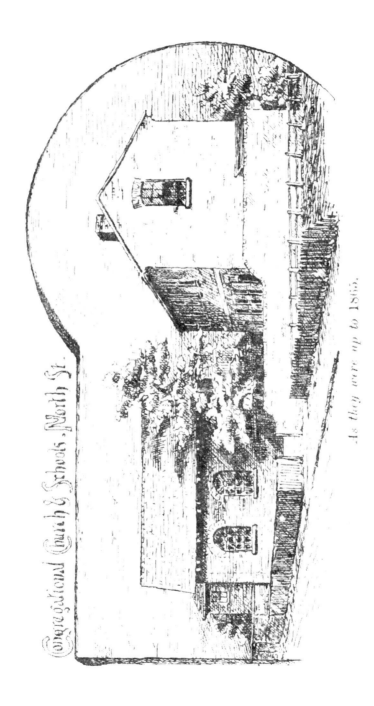

Congregational Church & Schools, North St.

As they were up to 1865.

Another day he took 15s. from a country dealer on the Essex Road. The man protested that it was his all. " I must have your money," said Turpin, " for I am hard up ; but take your stand in Newgate Street next Monday at noon, with your hat in your hand, and see what will happen." The man did as he was bid, and a stranger walking by dropped ten guineas into it. Then Turpin fascinated the people by his rapid rides. He would commit a robbery here and another forty miles off, in such a short space of time, that the populace almost credited him with supernatural powers. Turpin was born a century-and-a-half too soon. Had he lived in our time he would have been sent to the truant-school, his energies would have been turned in a right direction, and his splendid qualities might have found vent in Africa, where, as an explorer, he might have rivalled Stanley, and even Lord Randolph Churchill.*

Another visitor to Plaistow a few years after Turpin's execution was a man with a keen, pale face, and flowing locks that rested on his shoulders. See him mount his pony in the City Road, and canter along through Bow and Stratford. As he turns down West Ham Lane, he drops the reins, gives the pony her head, takes from his pocket a Latin treatise or his well-worn Greek Testament, and begins to read as he rides along. This is John Wesley, and he is coming to preach in the Broadway, In his diary are three records of visits to Plaistow. " Sept. 10th, 1739. I accepted a pressing invitation to go to Plaistow. At five in the evening I expounded there, and at eight again. But most of the hearers were very quiet and unconcerned. In the morning, therefore, I spoke stronger words. But it is only the voice of the Son of God which is able to awake the dead.—Monday, 17th. I preached again at Plaistow on ' Blessed are those that mourn.' It pleased God to give us in that hour two living instances of the piercing sense both of the guilt and power of sin, that dread of the wrath of God, and that full conviction of man's inability either to remove the power or atone for the guilt of sin.—Monday, 24th. I preached once more at Plaistow, and took my leave of the people of that place.

---

* An esteemed friend, holding an important public appointment in the Borough, who heard my lecture, writes to me that my treatment of Turpin is too lenient, and likely to relax the morals of the neighbourhood by setting such a career in an heroic light. The folly, wickedness, and futility of such a warring against society as Turpin practised are self-evident, and in these days when crime is so rapidly diminishing, it seemed scarcely necessary to dwell upon them.

cordially yours

John Curwen

On my return, a person galloping swiftly rode full against me, and overthrew both man and horse, but without any hurt to either. Glory be to Him who saves both man and beast."

This leads me to speak of the provision made for public worship in Plaistow. In the old days, West Ham Parish Church was the only place of worship. In the early part of the year 1796 the destitute state of the village engaged the notice of some Christian people at Stratford and Bow. They hired a room in Essex House in Greengate Street, and had it duly licensed for worship. Here the Rev. W. Newman (afterwards Dr. Newman), with the assistance of lay preachers, held two weekly services—one on Sunday evening, and the other on an evening in the week, until the year 1801. The room was then no longer available, and a Mr. Sparkhall, one of the supporters of the movement, who lived at Richmond House, lent a room attached to his house—an out-building which afterwards became a separate dwelling, and stood next to the butcher's shop adjoining. Students from Homerton College were engaged, and a stripling, who was afterwards celebrated as Dr. Raffles, of Liverpool, became very popular. In my time, there was in the courtyard of Richmond House a very large and lofty dog kennel, the top of which was formed by a massive slab of stone. I have often been told by my father that it was from this stone that Dr. Raffles preached on summer evenings when the congregation was too large to get into the room above. These services resulted in the building, in 1807, of the Independent Chapel in North Street. The chief promoters were Mr. Warmington, a Baptist, and Mr. R. H. Marten, an Independent, and the church became a union of both bodies. This church had a succession of able ministers; one of them, Mr. Lacey, is with us still in Lacey House, the last house on the right before the sewer bridge in Balaam Street. A full account of " The rise and progress of the Congregational Church, Plaistow, Essex; prepared and read at the Jubilee meeting, Oct. 18th, 1857, by Mr. John Burton," issued at the time as a pamphlet, gives information from which much that I have written is derived. I dwell on this movement because it represents the first attempt that was made at evangelising the village. Apparently it was not unneeded, for Mr. Burton records that the inhabitants broke the windows at the opening services, and that Mr. Marten, the chief promoter of the cause, received anonymous and threatening letters.

My father came to Plaistow in January, 1844, and was introduced to the pastoral charge of the Independent Chapel on May

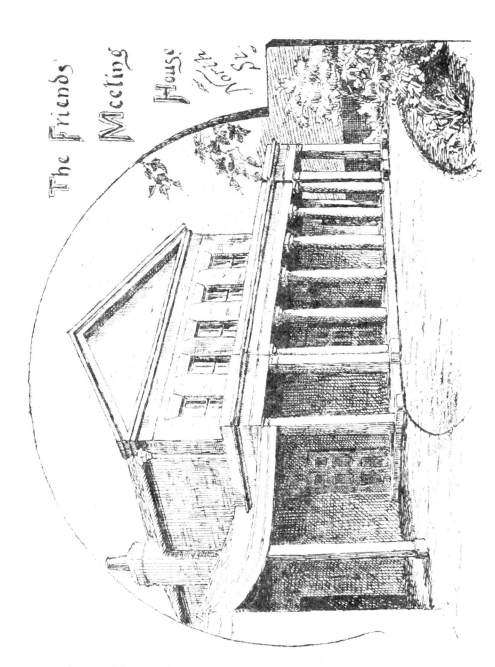

The Friends' Meeting House North St.

From a Photograph (kindly lent by Mrs. Godlee) taken shortly before
the building of the North Street Board Schools on this site.

22nd of that year. He at once began to make his influence felt, and his power over children and young people was especially marked. By Aug. 11th—seven months after his arrival—he had raised funds for and opened the public schools, and installed Mr. Alfred Brown as master. In many ways—religious, social, educational, political—he moved the village, and imparted to others his own high aims and enthusiasm. It is wonderful to think how the money was raised for the new Congregational Church (1859) and the schools by its side (1866). In all, I think, nearly £7,000 was collected. The effort was immense, and told upon him. He resigned the pastorate in 1864. His increasing responsibilities in connection with the Tonic Sol-fa movement combined with his pastoral work had for years made life a burden, and he would have lived longer if he had given up the pastorate earlier. When he first came to Plaistow, my father lodged for a month or two at Eastbourne House in Greengate Street with Mr. and Mrs. George Duck. On his marriage he moved to Woodbine Row, living afterwards in a house opposite, now pulled down; later at Linton House, and lastly at Richmond House. I cannot help mentioning also my mother's ceaseless activity on behalf of the poor. She lived for them. Apart from her household, this was her one enthusiasm, and occupied all her thoughts. In times of frost, or of special distress, her house became a soup kitchen, a clothes store, and a general relief office. With all this she was judicious and not easily imposed upon.

The Friends' meeting in North Street, now the board school, was built in 1819. There had been an older meeting-house at the back of the land. The stone pillars, still preserved, are from the Corinthian Portico of Wanstead House, one of the noblest houses, not only in England but in Europe, which was pulled down in 1822. Here in later years was heard, Sunday after Sunday, the saintly voice of Elizabeth Fry, who lived at the Cedars, in Portway. "More than once," writes Dr. W. M. Cooke, "I heard Mrs. Fry, and can bear testimony to the wholesomeness (I can find no better term) and dignity, almost majesty of her appearance, and to the wondrous music of her voice." In my boyhood, there were seldom less than twenty carriages, nearly all of them with a pair of horses, at the Friends' meeting on a Sunday morning. John Bright I have often seen there. I cannot resist bearing tribute to the good influence of the Friends upon Plaistow in old days. They were munificent supporters of schools and charities. The

Mrs. Fry in Newgate. From the "Band of Hope Review."

allotments question is still agitating rural England, but Samuel
Gurney solved it half-a-century since in this place, by setting aside
many acres of land around West Ham Park for the purpose. There
must have been one hundred allotments in all.

In 1825, a small Wesleyan Chapel, called Ebenezer Chapel, was
built in Greengate Street, close to the bottom of the garden of
Broadway House. It was promoted by Mr. Fisher, whose family
is happily still represented in Plaistow, and the members were very
good in visiting the sick. After some years, however, it was closed—

I am told the landlord seized it for unpaid ground rent—and was turned into two cottages, in which condition most of us remember it. The building was pulled down a few years ago to make room for shops. When the chapel closed, a gallery

St. Mary's Church. From the "Sunday at Home."

was built in the North Street Chapel, to accommodate the Wesleyans, who were homeless.

In 1830 St. Mary's Church was consecrated. Sir Henry Pelly, who lived in the Manor House, which stood at the top of Stopford Road, gave the site on condition that he should have a family vault. The builder was Mr. Thomas Curtis, husband of Mrs. Curtis, so well known as a bountiful property owner in the district, and the church is said to be the best piece of brickwork in the place.

In speaking of religious work, I cannot forbear a mention of the Misses Anderson, who lived in Balaam Street, nearly opposite the house where Edmund Burke lived. They were daughters of Captain Anderson, who received his commission from George III in the last century, and were both natives of Plaistow. The elder died 25 years ago, but the younger, Miss Sarah Anderson, lived until 1887. Both sisters were devoted to the poor, and to good works of every kind. Miss Sarah Anderson left no blood relations, and gave away all her money. She built a manse for the minister of the Congregational Church at a cost of £1,200, and did this during her lifetime, purchasing an annuity for herself at the same time. At her death my brother and I, as her executors, had to distribute a few legacies to personal friends, and were charged to give away the residue "for the good of Plaistow." We sent subscriptions to a number of societies of all denominations, and put up a drinking fountain opposite the "Abbey Arms" which will hand her name down to posterity.

Let us draw an imaginary picture of life in Plaistow at the beginning of the present century. Don't suppose that it was dull. The streets were more lively than they are now, for nearly every article was hawked, and the cries of the hawkers and pedlars, often quite musical, struck pleasantly on the ear. Baskets, chairs, door-mats, and brooms were carried from door to door; great piles of band boxes, brick-dust, and sand to put on the floor, lavender to put among the linen, watercresses, hot loaves, hot baked apples. Here is the knife-grinder's little cart; there is a man carrying rabbits on a pole. The girls of the Bonnell School at West Ham, in their mob caps and snowy pinafores, the boys in their yellow stockings and flat caps, flit about the streets. Dusk is coming on. The people straggle in from the fields, weary and hungry. No tea is drunk at the evening meal; beer is the universal beverage, and the very idea of doing without that would be preposterous. The tinder-box is brought out, and patiently we wait for a light to be struck and applied to a tallow candle, which serves at least to show how dark it is. Outside, the people—such as must be out—move to and fro with lanterns. If any have to go to West Ham, they make up a party, and carry one or two cudgels, as a protection against footpads. Meanwhile the fireside gossip begins. Very few can afford a newspaper, so news is spread by word of mouth, and this makes people sociable. A servant girl, home for a week from her place in the West End, tells how she has seen a shop in

Piccadilly lighted up not with lamps, but with a sort of gas that they say is made from coal. The listeners are horrified. Coal gas carried under the roads! The whole town will be poisoned or blown up. They are thankful they don't live in Piccadilly. This girl has a sister in service at Tunbridge Wells. When she comes home she takes the waggon, which does the 36 miles from London in 24 hours. The men form a group by themselves, and talk

Pulled down in 1881. *From a Photograph kindly lent by Mrs. Shrimpton.*

of the latest sport in cock-fighting and prize-fighting, as well as of the latest doings of the body-snatchers. Some tobacco is handed round, and bought by the men at a suspiciously cheap rate. If the truth were known it came from Holland in a Barking smack, was landed on the river wall in the dead of night, and has not paid duty. A group of young men are playing pitch and toss in the Broadway, under the dim light of an old lantern. What are those figures approaching them in the darkness? They are a party of blue-jackets, who, landing on the Essex side at the Poplar ferry, have tramped across the marsh silently and without a light. A scuffle, a shout, the click of the handcuffs, and half-a-dozen of the lads find themselves overpowered. They are in the hands of the press-gang, and in a month or two will be manning the ships of Nelson's fleet. Alas, for the sobbing mothers and sisters! Step into one of the big houses. There is a supper party, and two or three ladies have come to it in Sedan chairs. A merchant, just home from the city, relates that as he passed the Tower of London he saw flying the new royal standard with the harp of Erin added—a symbol of the union with Ireland which was just accomplished. A farmer, who has been at Romford Market, says that he passed the Ipswich coach on his way home, and saw it placarded " Peace with France," an item of news most important and eagerly discussed. The ladies in the drawing-room are canvassing points of dress. Hoops, they say, are going out, and some say that the towering wig is to come down. They chat further about the chances of the next Public Lottery at Cooper's Hall, and grieve over the death of a favourite young officer who was lately shot in a duel in Hyde Park. At nine the ladies go home; the gentlemen follow an hour or two later; two of them are fetched away helpless in a cart with clean straw at the bottom. The port wine of 1760 has been too much for them.

The government of Plaistow, even within the memory of men now living, was of the simplest. No drainage, no water, no street lights; everyone shifted for himself. "In 1844," says Mr. Henry Hay, "the only sewer in Plaistow was from near the church to the 'Abbey Arms,' where it emptied itself into an open ditch." The justices levied a highway rate on the property owners. There was a constable who lived in one of the houses in North Street, near St. Mary's Church. He had an assistant. This village constable wore no uniform, but he carried a brace of pistols, which were perhaps more impressive. The inhabitants of the big houses supported a night watchman, who went his rounds with a lantern, called the hour, and gave the weather. Behind where Nut Tree Terrace now stands was the village lock-up or cage, which I just remember. It was a small hut made of wood, bound round with iron hooping. There was a little hole in the wall, through which a friend could pass food to any drunken man who was confined there. The prisoners, when necessary, were marched off to Poplar. A prominent object on the river bank, just where the entrance to the Victoria Docks now is, was a gibbet, on which the bodies of cattle-lifters, pirates, &c., hung till they rotted away. The Friends refused, on conscientious grounds, to pay church rates, and once a year Mr. Cogan, the grandfather of Mr. George Hollamby, went in his official capacity and seized a piece of silver plate from Mr. Samuel Gurney at Ham House, and Mr. Fry at the Cedars. The franchise was high, and almost confined to the freeholders. At the general election of 1768 only four Plaistow electors went to Chelmsford to vote. The gratifying thing is that they all voted for the same two candidates. What a happy family we should be if we could all do that now! If you did not hold land, the only other chance for a vote was through a £60 rental, and as rents were low this class of voters was small. My father had no vote until he was well past 40 years of age. A Parliamentary election excited very limited interest. The people in general had no concern in it. Yet they managed to be happy without votes.

How did the people get to London? There was a stage coach driven by the grandfather of Mr. George Hollamby, return fare 3s. inside and 2s. outside. The people booked over night for this serious journey. Later on the fare was reduced, and then the coach was displaced by an omnibus, which ran to Leadenhall Market twice a day. But the best way of getting to London was to walk. One reason why the late Mr. Seale, of Plaistow Lodge, lived to such an advanced age was that for 20 years he walked to his business in London. About 1843 came the railway to Stratford Bridge. This was originally a coal tramway from Stratford to Blackwall Point, and it was afterwards continued to North Woolwich. The Plaistow line was not opened till 1859.

For many years Plaistow letters were carried to and from Stratford by two postmen. I remember that when the Tonic Sol-fa movement increased my father's correspondence, the General Post Office remonstrated with him for having so many letters, and said that the postmen could hardly carry them. They asked him to send them to Stratford. Mr. Perry tells me that often on a dark night the Plaistow postman of 40 years ago would see his cart standing in Stratford Broadway, come up to him and say, " I've only three or four letters for Plaistow; will you deliver them for me ? "

A yearly event in the village was the visit of the Lord Mayor, who drove from London by Stratford, through Plaistow, and back to town by the Barking Road and Iron Bridge. His visit was connected with the Thames Conservancy, and was abolished when the Conservancy was placed upon its present basis in 1857. This leads me to speak of the river walls. There is, I am told, no record of the present river walls being made. They are supposed to be the work of the Romans. As there is an Act of Parliament for repairing them as early as 1300, they must date back a long way. There are several old banks on the marshes, the longest of which crosses the Barking Road by Trinity Church. These banks, some people think, point to early attempts to dam in the river before the

Lodge and Gate of " The Willows" in old Plaistow Lane, near the Railway Station. The Gate and Fence from an Oil Painting by Mr. Wm. Thodey made some thirty years ago.

present banks were made. Near Cumberland House there is, or was, another piece of bank, called Pulley Wall, and in other parts of the marshes there are, or were, Monk's Pond, Waller's Pits, and Taylor's Hole, each of which have a mound or bank close to them, proving that they are artificial. We cannot be certain what is the history of these embankments, but they are certainly very old.

How was Plaistow educated in the old days? The first school was a Lancasterian school in a room in Porch House, which stood where Church Street joins High Street. The Quakers were its chief supporters. After a time it was closed, and in 1831 St. Mary's School was opened. A man named Oliver, who had been educated at the Bonnell School, gave money to build this Plaistow school. About 1840 the North Street Schools were established, and in 1843 Alfred Brown, whose name is so lovingly remembered, came to Plaistow. For forty-two years he was the master of these schools, and educated two generations of Plaistow boys and girls. At his death in 1885 there was universal regret. Such a gathering as that around his grave has probably not been equalled in Plaistow. In 1888 a tablet was erected, by old scholars, to his memory in the Balaam Street Schools with the following epitaph :—

> " We men that are, shew to the men to be
> A man who toiled for duty, not renown.
> His heart was true, his good done silently ;
> Let Plaistow hold in honour Alfred Brown."

Most of the middle-class boys of the last generation in Plaistow were educated at a small private school kept by Mr. Todd, in an old house in Balaam Street near Mr. Polley's shop, now pulled down.

In the first few years of the century an attempt was made to establish a fair in Plaistow. The fairs at Barking and at Bow were rowdy enough, and the Plaistow fair, after three years' trial, was put down by the magistrates in 1808. It was not suppressed without a riot; but special constables were sworn in, and order triumphed. In the broad space opposite the " Greengate Inn " there used to be sports at Easter, &c., climbing the greased pole, jumping in sacks, wheeling a barrow blindfold, and other intellectual occupations. Then there was a club feast, held for many years at the " Black Lion Inn." An old chaise without a bottom was dragged through the streets by the men on each feast day. Some tugged at the shafts, others balanced themselves on all its parts. At the large houses they stopped, gave three cheers, and waited for a tip. When the round of the village had been made, then came the supper.

Mrs. Robert Vause has lent me a very interesting fragment of a verbatim report of a trial which took place at the Assizes at Chelmsford arising out of some " rural sports " which were held at Plaistow on Whit Monday, 1809. Unfortunately the leaves of the report are incomplete, one or two pages being absent from

each end. I cannot, therefore, tell the exact nature of the indictment, nor the verdict of the jury, and though I have had the file of
the *Chelmsford Chronicle* for 1809-1810 searched, no report of the
case has been discovered. From the evidence I gather that from
1806 to 1809 it became the custom to have games in the Broadway
on Whit Monday. Each year the event attracted more people,
until the matter culminated in 1809. That year, as Whit Monday

As it was in 1800. From a Photograph kindly lent by Mr. Gardner.

approached, Mr. Robert Humphrey Marten, of Broadway House,
seems to have called a gathering of a few of the more respectable
inhabitants of the village, and as a result a bill was posted up
warning all persons that the attempt to establish a fair and games
was illegal. This bill was followed by a counterblast, calling on
the people to assemble and enjoy the games and races. Mr. Marten
and his supporters communicated with Mr. Manby, one of the
magistrates, and constables and peace officers from Woodford and
Barking, as well as from West Ham, assembled to stop the games
and disperse the assembly. Mr. Marten was mobbed because
he would not give half-a-crown to the sports, and the crowd

threatened to upset Farmer Adams' carriage for the same reason.
Two or three hundred persons assembled, and from 12 noon till 11
at night the disorder continued. The races seem to have been run
from the "Greyhound" to the "Black Lion." This, at least, was
the proposed course; but the constables caught hold of the com-
petitors as they started, and prevented them from running. One of
the races was for women. The trial does not seem to have been
brought about by the police, but by summons. The expenses were
paid apparently by Mr. Marten and other inhabitants, and the men
arraigned were simply defendants. The judge was Justice Heath;
the counsel for the prosecution Mr. Gurney, for the defence
Sergeant Best, with Messrs. Bolland, Garrow, and Adolphus as
juniors. The local witnesses for the prosecution were Farmer
James Adams, Mr. Ward (surgeon), Mr. William Rayner (baker
and churchwarden), Mr. Robert Humphrey Marten, Mr. Hagger,
Mr. William Plumb ("high constable of the parish of Plaistow"),
and Mr. Arthur Simms (gardener and constable). It is admitted
that three-fourths of the crowd were strangers to Plaistow. Farmer
Adams, a witness against the sports, was rather bowled over when
he had to admit that "his family had viewed them from a chamber
window." The trial was conducted in the most approved Old
Bailey style, with plenty of chaff, pumped-up indignation and
exaggeration by the Counsel. The aim of Sergeant Best was, of
course, to ridicule the whole affair as an attempt of the "Metho-
dists" to make everybody as glum as themselves. The riot, it will
be noticed, coincided with the opening of the Independent Chapel
(then the only place of worship in the village), and it is to this that
Sergeant Best refers, Mr. Marten having been the chief promoter
of the chapel. From the opening sentences of the judge's summing
up, it seems to me unlikely that the jury would convict the
defendants. I wonder who paid for the printing of this report?
It makes a pamphlet of nearly forty pages, and every word of the
evidence is given. From one or two foot-notes it is clear that
it emanates from the friends of the fair, and not from Mr. Marten's
side.

Two Plaistow characters of years ago are firmly printed in
mind. The first is Father Catton, a chemist in the Broadway,
a Friend, wearing the broad-brimmed hat, high collar, and great
white neckcloth, with which we are all familiar. His shop was like
a country store. He not only made up medicines, but was a linendraper, sold tin and ironware, earthenware and sweets. Father

Father Catton.   From the "Band of Hope Review,"
about 1855.

Catton was the first abstainer I ever heard of in Plaistow. He had
a magic lantern, and used to delight us children with his pictures
and his humour. He built the temperance hall in North Street,
now St. Mary's Mission Hall, and brought the first drinking
fountain to Plaistow.

Temperance Hall, North Street. From the "Sunday at Home."

The second character is a different one—Joe Duck. His father kept the "Black Lion" before the late Mrs. Cohu, and was a farmer as well. Joe always dressed in a fashionable style, wore a large flower in his button-hole, and carried a hoe as a walking stick. He was a cricketer, and I remember an oil painting of him standing before the wicket in white ducks and a chimney-pot hat. For years he never missed seeing an execution at Newgate. Every Sunday he walked to the "Spotted Dog" and dined there. Once he got into a dispute with Canon Ram, the vicar of West Ham, which he described as a conflict between the horned and the feathered tribes. The name was a peculiar one. A Plaistow magnate, driving along the lane, was stopped by a litter of little pigs, which were all over the place. "Whose pigs are these?" he cried to a boy standing near. "They're Duck's, sir," was the reply, and the poor boy, who only spoke the truth, got a cut of the whip for his pains. Joe Duck had a great belief in cold water; at any rate, for external application. I can see him now, standing at his door in

his shirt sleeves, polishing his face with the towel till it shone like
the sun.   He was a freeholder, and at election times was in great
force.   Duck's Fields, at the bottom of Whitwell Road, belonged to
him, and George. Charles, and Jane Streets there, are named after

Pulled down 1875.   *Drawn from a Photograph kindly lent by
Mr. Thos. Cohu.*

his children.   In his latter years Joe had a tussle with the parish
authorities.   I fancy they made up a road on his property, for
which work he declined to pay.   He shut himself up in his house,
put a lattice in front of his door, and " Joe Duck's Castle," in
Richmond Street, was a joke for everybody.   On Sundays he was
free, and would eat his dinner in the front garden to remind
the public of the fact.

But I must not ramble further. I fear I have been too long already. My work to-night has not been to collect matter, but to compress it and leave it out. London, when it came, came with a rush, and swamped the old village of Plaistow. The increase of population is, I suppose, scarcely paralleled in the country. In 1801 there were only 6,485 people in the whole of West Ham parish, and so slow was the increase, that in 1841 there were only 12,738. After that the parish filled up by leaps and bounds, and the subsequent ten-year censuses have shown, in round numbers—18,000, 37,000, 62,000, 128,000, and 204,000. This is for the whole parish. In the Plaistow Ward there were, as late as 1861, only 11,214 people; now there are 80,000. The increase has been due to several causes. About 1847 the Thames Iron Works came across the river; the docks and other industries followed; the wild fowl forsook the marshes, and their place was taken by miles of streets. The Plaistow railway helped the growth, and the old agricultural village became part of the mighty metropolis. The immigration was tremendous. At the census of 1881 West Ham parish showed 128,953 inhabitants, of whom only 49,484 were born within the county of Essex. Making allowance for the immigration from the rural parts of Essex, which is considerable, that means that in 1881 two out of every three men, women, and children living in West Ham were not born there. The figures for 1891 are not yet out, but the proportions will probably be only slightly altered. This fact explains a good deal of the aimlessness and want of order which characterise the municipal and political life here. The people do not know or trust one another. New comers neither know or care about the past, and are always wanting to make a fresh start. But all this will mend. The forces making for enlightenment were never so strong as they are now. Not only are the churches full of religious activity, but they are tackling the social question in a splendid way, and offering occupation for weekday leisure as well as for Sunday. The day and Sunday schools are doing better work each year; recreation grounds and free libraries are in the air. The old times are gone never to return. The ploughman, the grazier, the marshman, have given place to the artisan, the city clerk, the factory hand. Let us see to it, that while carrying forward all that was best in old Plaistow, we set our faces ever for progress, for brotherhood, for human development in its highest and best form.

APPENDIX (A).

RECOLLECTIONS OF PLAISTOW, BY THE REV. R. W. B. MARSH, **M.A.**, INCUMBENT AND VICAR, 1842 to 1884.

FROM the close connection which has been formed between Plaistow and its neighbourhood with my family, which has lasted through three generations, I have ever felt a warm interest in all its concerns, and willingly jot down two or three trifling incidents of long ago. My father came to live in Plaistow in the year 1799. A very primitive village it was then; out of the world, it led nowhere; it was what Lancashire people call a poke (or pocket), a way in, no way out. It was his first start in life as a surgeon. His home was in Balaam Street, one of the houses which at the present time are being docked of their front gardens. He soon gathered a few patients. Amongst the houses he visited was a ladies' school (Mrs. Eyre's, the Manor House in High Street), at which my mother was at that time a parlour-boarder. In due time he robbed that establishment of what no doubt he considered its greatest ornament, and I should certainly be the last to gainsay it. But before this event, he had found that Plaistow was too healthy for him, and he removed to Stratford, where a medical practitioner had more chance, in prolonging the lives of others, of prolonging his own. Still, for divers reasons, his favourite practice was in Plaistow. He liked the people and their ways, and I well remember how as a boy I used to accompany him when he went to visit his patients. If the day were very fine, he used to leave me with my kite in the field near the old workhouse, where there was then only one cottage near—a lodge to the farm. A young boy alone was not likely to remain long unmolested. Strong rough field boys—giants in my estimation—would molest me, and try to snatch my kite away. One day four or five of them gathered round me, and asked my name. I had been reading one of Shakespeare's historical plays, and I answered resolutely that I was the Duke of Bedford! It was very wrong of me. I noticed with surprise their awe-stricken countenances. What ideas they had about dukes I do not know; but I suppose they thought them grand and powerful. The result was, " they went their way," as John Bunyan says, and I saw them no more, nor was I ever molested again. I suffered, however, for my deceit; I never entered that field without feeling that my imposture might be found out, and I should reap the consequences. Sometimes I went with my father to the houses of his patients; he always attended the Piegromes. How well I remember that old house which had then been in their possession nearly 100 years! What a sight it was! The old father and his four sons all as busy as busy could be—John, Edmund, Jerry, and James—tongues and hands keeping equal pace. How my eyes wandered from one to another—the blind mother rocking in her chair. I was a bit of a favourite of them all, and long after I was ordained, some of them still called me Master Bishop. Then again, how often have I visited Father Catton. My father *always* attended his family—a family of 13 or 14—and I did not come away from his miscellaneous shop empty. Mr. Vause, too, a life-long inhabitant, my boyhood initiated a life-long friendship with him. Using the term life-long reminds me what long lives the people of those days attained to. I wonder whether many can say that they have buried five centenarians, yet such is the case with me. And how they retained their bodily strength to the end! I well remember with what gusto my father would tell the tale of a woman nearly a hundred years old, a field worker—that occupation made them so strong—Mrs. Pig, I believe her name was. She had every half-year to go for some allowance or pension to Bethnal Green. As she returned by Bonner's fields, a terribly lonely road, two men stopped her and tried to take from her her money. She raised her fists, knocked them both down, and arrived safely home. When my father asked her if she were not afraid at her age, she indignantly answered, " Afeard of them— do you think I was going to give up my money to those whipper-snappers ! " Another tale some years later :—Mrs. Marsh was visiting an old woman, who said to her, " I cannot tell what's the matter with my daughter there ; she sits in her chair, and I can hardly move her to help me in the house work." This said daughter was only 80 years old ; her mother was 102. Many will remember Mrs. Ireland, who lived to her hundredth year. I saw her not long before her departure, and she was so cheerful and well, that I quite thought she would have overstepped the 100 years. In her garden was a wonderful pear tree, twice her own age. Every bough was clad in ivy, and yet produced a quantity of pears. An artist in Plaistow took a pen and ink sketch of it and gave it to me. I fear, like all other trees, it will disappear.

Now for locomotion. It seems but the other day that Covell's omnibus used to ply round the (then) village, and take up passengers for the distant city. The horn gave notice of its approach, and hurried sluggards had to dispatch their dressing or their breakfast. Three times a day did it go; I remember the joyous excitement when the three was extended to four. It took its time ; why make a toil of a pleasure ? I remember one day, as it turned into Balaam Street for its usual course through Stratford, I started walking to go by the Commercial Road, a somewhat shorter distance. When I reached Whitechapel Church, I had to wait five minutes for its arrival. The Plaistow of to-day surely cannot be the same Plaistow. Oh, as the trees were ruthlessly cut down, one after another, how my heart ached ! It was like losing a friend. As the prolific gardens, famous for mulberry trees, abounding in choice fruit trees of every description, were metamorphosed into a colony of streets. What ? We could only sigh and try to be resigned. There were horticultural shows in Wanstead Park in those days, and many were the prizes that were claimed by Plaistow. And wild flowers ! I remember, in an address to children, telling them that one day in Palsy Lane I had picked twenty-five different flowers. In the ditch near the Abbey Mills was to be found the large bright water forget-me-nots, the surface of the ditch emulating the sky above in pureness of colour. In the Vicarage garden in Howards Road we dug down and came upon pipes which used to feed a large fish-pond. In my garden in Balaam Street numerous singing birds of various sorts tamely came to our window to be fed. One year, a great pleasure, the trees in my garden attracted a nightingale, and owls occasionally haunted my church. I have not quite done with Father Catton. I feel almost sure that he induced Father Matthew to come to Plaistow and proclaim his crusade. He was the earliest promoter of teetotalism. Almost—need I say almost—all children loved Father Catton; but children will be rough occasionally, and un-tamed, and a boy threw a stone at him (this I witnessed), which wounded his mouth severely. I was about to take hold of the boy, but Father Catton forestalled me, and went up to him and said, in such gentle tones, "My boy, in a few minutes you will be sorry for this." He would have borne, he would not have cared for, reproof; but this was too much for him; he burst into tears. I wonder whether anyone remembers a strong, stalwart woman named Betty Parker. When quite old she could carry with ease a sack of coals; she used to go round with coals and greengrocery. There was in that woman, rough as she was, a great overflow of kindly feeling. She introduced herself to me the first morning after I arrived at Plaistow, by standing at my gate and crying out in a loud masculine voice, "I sells taters." And she did sell "taters" to us as long as she sold "taters" at all. She ended her life in the Union; but there was a little pleasant romance in that, for she went the same day with one who had been her companion as a child in Bonnell's School, and with whom she had kept up affectionate intercourse ever since.

Who did not know well our ancient doctor (Dr. Beale) and his amiable wife; how many a notable woman would she scold, and how humbly they bore their scolding, for they knew well what would come after. She was a great stickler for due etiquette, and yet she told me that a few years before I arrived at Plaistow, she could walk without a bonnet to see her neighbours, so primitive was the village. When first I came to Plaistow, the house where the too famous Dr. Dodd lived had been made into two houses, which were respectively tenanted by Miss Bell (a Quaker lady) and myself. I then had pupils to prepare for Cambridge. I remember hearing one of them singing out lustily, "Merrily dance the Quaker's wife, and merrily dance the Quaker," quite oblivious of our next-door neighbour. When I called on her, I was offering an apology, but she stopped me, and said she heard it and was very much amused. Do any

remember a very tall, gentlemanly, kind-hearted man, very fond
of children, a very useful man in the parish, intelligent, practical?
This was Mr. Alfred Robinson; he lived in the house which
the great statesman, Burke, once visited. When Plaistow began
to increase, he asked if it would not be a good thing to prevent the
old inhabitants from being altogether forgotten by giving their
names to the new streets. Through him, therefore, we have so
many streets named after the old inhabitants—Webb Street, Sewell
Street, Kelland Road, Warmington Street, Beale Street, Riles
Street, Swete Street, and others. He was very perplexed how to
perpetuate my name, for Marsh Street would simply convey the
idea that it led to the Plaistow Marshes. I waved the distinction,
nor did I find out till some time after that he had got out of
his difficulty by naming one of them Bishop Road, from one of my
Christian names. This I thought rather misleading, for it might be
thought to have been the seat of a bishop, there being an abbey so
near. There was one school in Balaam Street for the young
gentlemen of the village. This for many years was conducted by
Mr. Todd. As to the Irish colony in Greengate Street and Greengate Yard, I rather liked the Irish; there was so much humour
in their talk. I fear they were not many of them disciples
of Father Matthew, and they were rather fond of a quarrel. As
Mrs. Marsh and I were walking across the Broadway on one
occasion, two of them were taking off their upper clothes to fight;
I went up to them, and said, "It is very wrong to fight." "So it
is, your reverence; Bill, put your jacket on." And away they
went. In our evening school many big Irish boys attended, and
when the school was over, I used to play a few simple airs on the
accordion, which always amused them; but as the last, they always
insisted on having "The conversation I heard between the Monument and St. Paul's," and they would join, if not in melodious, in
very enthusiastic chorus, and would go shouting it down the street.
Those boys were very fond of me, and I of them.

APPENDIX (B).

THE ATTEMPTED FAIR (p. 37).

THE trial was entitled "The King v. John Cochran and others," an indictment for conspiracy and riot. Mr. Garrod, the counsel, in opening the case, regretted that the defendants had not given the prosecutors an opportunity of settling the case out of court. He said that his clients had no objection to innocent sports, but objected to their worship being interrupted by violence and insult, and the sanctity of their private dwellings being violated. He also mentioned the receipt of a threatening letter, which might have been made the subject of a capital charge. The judge (Justice Heath), in summing up, said there was no evidence of an attempt to establish a fair, nor of a riot. Donkey races, women racing for shifts, and the variety of diversions which had been described in the evidence, were not rioting. The defendants should have been simply indicted for a nuisance. The jury immediately, on the judge's recommendation, found the defendants not guilty. The printer of the pamphlet is G. Barber, 16, Fleet Street, London. I gather these particulars from a complete copy of the report of the trial kindly lent me by Mr. Strutt, of High Street.

DR. DODD (p. 12).

"Lord Chesterfield's Letters to his Godson," published under the editorship of the Earl of Carnarvon in 1889, contains four letters addressed "To Master Philip Stanhope, at Dr. Dodd's house at West Ham in Essex." These are all of the year 1766. On Sept. 6th, 1766, Lord Chesterfield writes to Philip Stanhope's father:—"The Doctor and he go at Michaelmas to settle in their new house at Great Russell Street, Bloomsbury." In another letter he speaks of Dr. Dodd as "the best and most eloquent

E

preacher in England, and perhaps the most learned clergyman. He is now publishing notes upon the whole Bible, as you will see in the advertisements in many of the newspapers."

A PLAISTOW CELEBRITY.

Aaron Hill, a man of good family and leisure, who dabbled in many things, from poetry to potash, and the theatre to timber, married the daughter of Mr. Edmund Morris, of Stratford, and settled at Plaistow in 1738, remaining there till his death in 1749. He wrote the libretto of the opera *Rinaldo* which Handel set to music. He was the friend of Alexander Pope, and being a generous man, gave the proceeds of his books to the relief of poor persons. He interested himself in the question of extracting oil from beech-nuts, and in 1728 went to the Highlands of Scotland, where he found timber for the Royal Navy, and succeeded in floating it down the Sprey, to the astonishment of the natives. After retiring to Plaistow, he occupied himself with his children and his garden, experimenting in the art of making potash, which was then not much understood in England. He was buried in the cloisters of Westminster Abbey.

ANOTHER PLAISTOW CELEBRITY.

In "Worthies of Essex" there is a portrait and sketch of George Edwards, F.R.S., F.S.A., an eminent naturalist, born April 3rd, 1693, at Stratford-le-Bow. He travelled much; wrote a famous "History of Birds," which he dedicated to "The Supreme Being." The plates were exactly coloured from nature. He also wrote "Gleanings in Natural History." He retired to Plaistow, and died there July 23rd, 1773, aged 80. A plain stone in West Ham Churchyard commemorates his talents as artist and geologist.

CAN ANY GOOD COME OUT OF PLAISTOW?

The scarcely feigned surprise which some reviewers of this pamphlet have shown in the discovery that there is actually a place in the East End of London which possesses antiquarian and personal interest, is amusing. Plaistow, I suppose, has always contributed its fair share to the notabilities of the day. In my own time, for example, it has produced Dr. J. S. Reid, one of the leading tutors and classical scholars at Cambridge; Mr. W. Biscombe Gardner, who is an easy first among our wood engravers; and Miss Mabel Harrison, whose skill as an elocutionist has won the warmest praise from Mr. Henry Irving. Sir Joseph Lister, known all the world over as the discoverer of the antiseptic treatment, which has revolutionised operative surgery, was brought up at Upton House.

PLAISTOW IN 1821-1836.

A lady, who wishes her name withheld, writes :—I think that I first went to reside with my parents at Plaistow in 1821 or 1822, and we lived opposite to Jane Warmington, not very far from the "Abbey Arms" public-house, which was then noted for prize-fighters coming there, as they could so readily pass over to the Isle of Dogs, which was in the county of Middlesex. It was a great pleasure to me as a child to watch the Lord Mayor and Sheriffs, who came down once a year to review the banks of the Thames. The old Friends' Meeting House was still in existence then, and was almost close to the street. My grandfather's premises had a door into the yard adjoining it. He went to reside there in 1780, and died in 1806. It was a square built house, standing a little way back in the garden, with a coach-house and stable, with small croft and large garden, to which Rayner's (the baker's), the Cage, Moss (the blacksmith), a plumber and glazier, and Samuel Catton's shop, &c., formed the boundary, and the Meeting House yard, the other abutting into the premises of the "Black Lion," and two or three intervening cottages. Thus it formed the centre of "the island," as we used to call it. Having lost my parents, I went to reside with my aunt in the half of Dr. Dodd's house about 1830, when it was reported to be haunted, but no inconvenience arose from this, save a very low knocking occasionally at night in the wall of different rooms. A few weeks after a mouse was caught with a bony excrescence on one leg, which, no doubt, occasioned the noise, as it was heard no more. I believe Luke Howard left Plaistow before we went there, but I remember Howard's pump very well. I do not think there was a scarcity of water in Plaistow, but this well was made much deeper than the others in order to get a softer water for the benefit of the laundresses, &c., and was very much frequented. I never heard that Benjamin West resided in Plaistow, but Samuel West did so for some years, and the summer-house drawn in thy book is exactly like one in his garden. He had a turning-lathe, and being of a studious mind often spent a good deal of time in the summer-house. His death was a very sad one, for, driving Charles Marten home from a committee, his sight being bad,

he drove on to the bank at a turn in West Ham Lane. Both
gentlemen were thrown out just as a waggon was passing ; the wheel
went over Samuel West's head and Charles Marten's hair, who had
a severe illness afterwards from the great shock. I was very
pleased to find Samuel Catton so kindly noticed in thy book. He
was very much respected, and a warm promoter of the Temperance
cause. He came down to Alton at my request to show his magic
lantern to the juvenile Temperance Society. The Misses Anderson,
too, I was pleased to hear of, and think they did credit to old
Plaistow. I remember the building of the church at the corner of
Palsy Lane. The clock was given by our cousin, Samuel Gurney,
but went very badly. I never found many wild flowers in Palsy
Lane, but the nightingale sang there, and in Upton Lane. The
flowering rush grew very freely in the ditches in the marshes. The
larvæ of the goat moth was a disagreeable looking creature, when,
at the end of three years, it gnawed its way out to find a place
suitable to turn into a chrysalis. It was dark brown above, and
salmon colour underneath, and emitted a strong odour like a goat.
I never succeeded in obtaining a specimen of the perfect insect. I
used to call on a poor woman in Pinnock's Place, and went to see
old Mrs. Pig in Plaistow Lane, who kept a small needle and fine
cotton in a bottle on the chimney-piece in order to show how good
her sight was at 100 years, by threading the needle in her visitor's
presence. I remember the name of Mr. Lacey, as minister at the
chapel, and Mr. Munro gave us lessons in Latin. Mr. Temple was
a very pleasant gentleman, residing there when we left Plaistow in
1836. I knew R. H. Marten and Charles Marten and his wife very
well.

MR. HARRY RAND'S RECOLLECTIONS.

Mr. Harry Rand has been in Constantinople for twenty-six
years, yet his recollections of old Plaistow are very vivid, as the
following paper shows. Mr. Rand's father was a marshman, and
through him his information goes back a long way :—

I very well remember our family coming to Plaistow in the
summer of 1839, some trivial circumstances connected with the
moving being much better remembered than more important
matters of a later date. You mention in your pamphlet the Rev.
Mr. Bosanquet. From what I can call to mind, I think he must
have been unpopular, for on the Rev. Mr. Sims taking his place
many more people attended church. We occupied one of those

two cottages opposite the old chapel in North Street, the gardens of which became Smith's building-yard. Here, of course, I became well acquainted with Pinnock's Place, as our back pathway led into it. At that time the old houses in Pinnock's Place were mostly occupied by Irish families. A Miss Harper kept a school in the room between Bright's shop and Richmond House, to which my mother sent me for some time until I was considered capable of holding my own in the National School (Oliver's).

Plaistow Temperance Hall was built in 1840, and opened on 20th August of that year. My father became one of the first members of the Plaistow Total Abstinence Society. He signed the pledge on the 21st, the second night, and I am thankful to say remained a staunch teetotaler until he died in 1885. Dear old Father Catton was the prime mover in the good work, and how he managed to get money enough, by voluntary subscriptions, for the purpose of building a temperance hall in those beer-loving days has always been something of a mystery to me, although I know his chief supporters were the Gurney and Buxton families. While I am on this theme, a saintly figure rises up before my mind, in the tall cap and glossy brown silk dress that covered that dear lady, Rebecca Sturges. She followed in the wake of Mrs. Fry, and did the same blessed work. I have heard those say whom she has visited in sickness, that her cheery " How art thou, dear ? " has infused, as it were, new life into them.

I wonder how many there are living who remember. Palsy Lane as it was in the early forties, with here and there a cow or two grazing on the herbage growing along the broad parts, or standing under the trees which grew on the meadow side of Robinson's pond nearly up to their bellies in water, chewing the cud of contentment. We boys of St. Mary's (Oliver's) School were wont to bathe there in summer and slide in winter. Again, who remembers Tommy Ruffet's House, that stood on the right hand side of Palsy Lane where it joined the lane leading from Plashet Park Lodge (at the end of Gipsy Lane) to what we boys knew as Morley's Castle, for Green Street only extended from the tower to Barking Road. I very well remember the Ruffets, and the old house too ; it was certainly in a dilapidated state, and was pulled down when the Ruffets left it. I must say I have something of Mr. Marsh's feeling about those splendid oak, elm, and ash trees being ruthlessly cut down. Look to any point of the compass, from your perch on any field gate in Palsy Lane, and trees, lovely trees, were seen, most of which I have climbed, either for bird's nests or for shinty sticks. But no statement of Palsy Lane of that time would be perfect without a reference to the Priest family. The old house stood in the garden, the gateway being almost hidden by a most luxurious privet on each side and meeting overhead. You will no doubt call to mind the old lady with her wheelbarrow loaded with what she used to hawk as " taters, greens, and wegablls." They were a very strange old couple, and kindly to a fault, in particular the old gentleman; but I am afraid there is but little left now to remind even an old stager of the Palsy Lane of 50 years ago.

At the time of which I am writing Sir J. H. Pelly was living, and cultivated the land on each side of Plashet Road (Portway). I can well remember what a nicely kept farmyard Pelly's was. Sir Henry was in the habit of distributing Christmas comforts to poor people on Christmas morning, but the custom ceased when he died, much to the grief of some of the old folks, who have long since passed away too.

One cannot speak of Dr. Beale without bringing to mind old Joe Duck, publican and farmer, and the " Black Lion " yard with its loads of fresh vegetables packed ready for market. I can very well remember the old gent in cord breeches, brown coat, and rather broad-brimmed hat. There must have been some ill-feeling between him and his son Joe, for I remember Joe burning his father's effigy in the field which is now crossed by the railway before it crosses Upton Lane.

Bull-baiting was carried on in the Broadway in former days. I have heard my father speak of it; but it was not in his day. Mr. Vause's original shop stood back in a line with Catton's and Maywood's places, until he built the house and shop that was standing 26 years ago, perhaps is now.

Near the " Abbey Arms," on the left facing the Iron Bridge, is Forty Acre Lane, at the corner of which stood the Pound, where stray cattle of any kind were put and kept until released by their owners paying poundage. This lane led by Cherry Island, which was a sort of small market gardener's, the place in all probability taking its name from the cherry trees that were planted round the piece of land at the back of the house. A wide ditch ran all round outside the trees. This lane ran as far as where the " Hallsville Tavern " stands, or near that spot; there is a narrow creek running as far as the Stores in the Thames Iron Works (out of Bow Creek). This is the commencement of a very wide shaw; these shaws, of which there were a good number about the marshes, were the source of supply to the smaller ditches. This particular shaw ran all through the Plaistow Marshes on the upper side of Prince Regent Lane. The principal shaw on the lower side of Prince Regent Lane, and communicating with East Ham Marshes, was called Creek Head Shaw. This shaw was supplied directly from the Thames by a sluice under the river wall. This brings me to say something about these walls, or, as you have called them in your pamphlet, banks. I leave out of the question the river walls, as it was only the river walls that were protected by Act of Parliament. Those you mention as Pulley Wall, &c., were known as County walls, and, according to marshmen's tradition, were thrown up to keep back the water from the lower lands in very high spring tides when there was no other check, such as the sluice before mentioned. The wall you mention, that crossed the Barking Road near Trinity Church, was a continuation of Pulley Wall; this wall protected all that area from Bushey Acre, where the wall ended, by Waller's Pits, across the Barking Road, away into what is now Hallsville, and keeping more or less the course of the shaw until it merged into Pulley Wall proper and came down to Mrs. Ireland's farmyard. There was another County wall running nearly parallel with Prince Regent Lane; this guarded the Plaistow side of Creek Head Shaw, and near the piece of water mentioned as Monk's Pond, known as Mugg's Pond. Dr. Taylor's hole was guarded by the Bow Creek river wall, Waller's Pits by Bushey Acre Bank, and Mugg's Pond as above. As a boy I learned to swim in Dr. Taylor's Hole, by taking a header into the stream that ran through a cast iron pipe at high water in the Abbey branch of Bow Creek. Of course, as soon as confidence in my buoyancy was established, Dr. Taylor's Hole was discarded for the Creek or Waller's Pits, where there was more room. Mugg's Pond had an evil repute, as several people committed suicide there. I call to mind one, an ostler at the " Green Gate " of the name of Hobbs, who drowned himself there about 38 years ago, as near as I can judge. Mugg's Pond was about half-way between where the marshes commenced and the " Prince Regent Tavern." I well remember this house. It was quite a resort for sportsmen, and shooting matches were often held there. It was also a ferry house from Charlton on the Kent side. There were many lanes, or bridle ways, called so from the fact that they were not thoroughfares, but led to certain marshes, from which they generally, though not always, took their names; for example, Star Lane, leading from Forty Acre Lane, by Mrs. Mason's ladies' school, crossing the Barking Road, and finishing at Starr Pound, or Cow Bridge Marsh. There was a very nice lane leading from Pulley Wall called Green Lane; this finished at a three-acre field. There were some nice trees and bushes along Green Lane, and it well merited its name. I had no idea that Hudson Farm was ever connected with Royalty (Cumberland House). In the early forties Richard Hudson lived there, and cultivated the land. He was called "Dick of the Dicks," but why I do not know. I distinctly remember his death; the land was then taken, some by Mrs. Ireland and some by Mr. Adams. A family of the name of Austin lived there after Hudson's. I think they were related to Hudson, but am not sure. After them came the Kellands.

Teams of bulls or oxen were quite common in those days. Mr. Adams had one team of four splendid shorthorn bulls; they were generally used in ploughing, or in the mill where chaff was cut, or water pumped for washing potatoes, carrots, turnips, greens, &c.

I can well remember the first threshing machine coming. Many a time I have stood and watched the threshers with the flail; my father was something of a don in the making of a flail.

About 1842 or 1843, Richard Gregory, of Woodgrange Farm, died, and Mr. William Adams took it. He made many improvements in farming. He had, I believe, the first threshing machine, and sealed the doom of the flail in West Ham parish. It was considered a wonderful invention, and doubtless was. But that great lumbering affair was but the embryo of the present machine, that cleans the corn and ties the straw too. However, I am straying from Plaistow to Forest Gate.

When our family first came to Plaistow, a Mr. Temple preached at North Street Chapel. One of my aunts belonged to his congregation, and was in the habit of walking from Upton Place every Sunday afternoon to hear him preach. From what I picked up in hearing her speak of him, I thought Mr. Temple must be something better than a man.

At the time of which I am writing, the Ancients were the business people of Plaistow, such as Dr. Beale and Joe Duck's father. Mr. Rudall kept the linendraper's shop, Timothy Surry (John's father) kept the baker's shop next to Rudall's, which, ultimately, Mr. Geo. Duck occupied. Mr. Benton was in Boddy's, McPherson's nursery was all aglow with flowers, Abraham and

Isaac Cumbers worked the ground that Goodman had when I left Plaistow, Mayhew's had the livery stables that Mr. Sam Covil ran the omnibus from. There was also a corn-chandler's shop attached. Covil afterwards took the " Coach and Horses ; " Mrs. Rayner remained in the old shop in High Street (vide p. 33). I never knew Mr. Rayner. Robert Trott kept the " Green Gate," and Tom Merry the "Abbey Arms." In Balaam Street, before those shops where Hislop, Edridge, and Mrs. Stewart were in business, had the fronts run out, the grocer's was opposite, where Miss Wheeler had her school, and was kept by a Mr. Palmer. I have also a misty recollection of old Mr. Gwalter, the father of Ephraim and Toby, who, I doubt not, you will remember something of. Higher up, and where the sewer crosses the street, was Mr. Rayner's general shop. He also ran the carrier's cart before our old friend Mr. Hugh Perry took it. You, of course, will remember Perry's place near the Abbey Arms, and lower down Stouard's smithy and wheelwright's place; waggon building in those days was no mean trade. I very well remember old Mr. Cobley, of Cobley Hall, at the corner of Forty Acre Lane.

There is no doubt about old Plaistow being famous for its cattle feeding. Mr. King, who lived in the house occupied by Mr. Thos. Roberts, made a business of it. Hence the meadows abreast of North Street were called King's fields, a Mr. Spurling acted for King as my father did for Tucker. King was continually trying some experiments with different kinds of food stuffs, and I remember Sam Spurling (son of the above) telling my father that King fatted an ox on treacle, hay, and swedes, so that it could not be got through the door of the shed without removing the door frame.

My mouth waters when mention is made of the fruit trees of dear old Plaistow, such Ribstone, five crown, Chester and Quarantine pippins. I never saw these equalled anywhere else. The best Quarantines were in Dr. Beale's garden. I cannot forbear to mention a famous pear tree that grew in a paddock nearly opposite Essex Lodge, into which was grafted six different kinds of pears. It yielded its fruit from the earliest to the latest. But I must stop. Perhaps I am a bit of an enthusiast when Plaistow is the theme, for I love the old place.

Mr. Reed's Recollections.

I have had an interesting talk with Mr. Reed, of Church Street, about old times in Plaistow. His father settled here as a thatcher in 1818, and the son, who was born in Plaistow in 1824, has followed the trade ever since. Thatching is not so common as it was, but Mr. Reed is known as one of the best hands in the country, and is called here and there to thatch summer houses, and the lodges of large parks. Mr. Reed says that Howard's pump was erected in 1807. There was a date upon the under side of the leaden top. He was once called in to repair it, and on sounding found a distance of 18 feet to the water, and 36 feet from the top of the water to the bottom; total, 54 feet. The usual depth for wells in Plaistow had been about 10 feet. The barn at the back of Cumberland House, he says, is 130 feet long, and the surface measurement of the roof from eaves to apex is 50 feet. The barn, he believes, is not made of horse chestnut, but of Spanish chestnut, a wood that is as lasting as oak. Mr. Reed always heard that the Danes built the river walls, and that long ages ago the tide flowed up to the "Abbey Arms," but not within a quarter-of-a-mile of the "Green Gate." Old Danish tobacco-pipes, so small that one could hardly get one's little finger inside, used constantly to be dug up near the surface. There was an old house where the "Victoria Tavern" now stands in High Street, pulled down in 1856. It was built of wood, and had 12 or 14 rooms. In New Barn Street there was another old wooden house, pulled down about 1830. In Green Gate Street, where two houses now stand with gardens in front, there was another old house, also pulled down about 1830. Mr. Lennox, who had an anchor and cable factory at Millwall, had a house opposite the "Greyhound," which was pulled down in 1844. Mr. Reed also recalls the old house which stood in Greengate Street between the two houses named above and Cable's Yard. Here for a long time lived Mr. and Mrs. Roberts, warm-hearted and intelligent Scotch people. Mr. Roberts was a mahogany broker in London, and was a man of much vigour and grasp of mind. Everyone in Plaistow knew him. Mrs. Roberts was most benevolent to the poor, and was universally beloved. Like most of the old Plaistow houses this had a stone post on the curb, to enable ladies to mount a horse or to step into the pillion saddle behind their cavalier. Mr. Reed says that in his early days from whichever side Plaistow was approached the village was concealed by large elm trees, which shrouded it in green.

Mrs. Adams' and Miss Ireland's Recollections.

Mrs. Adams and Miss Ireland, whose acquaintance I have made since the first edition of this pamphlet was issued, are sisters who represent two of the very oldest and most influential Plaistow families. I wish I had known, before writing my paper, that they were still in Plaistow. In the old days, the chief wealth of Plaistow was derived from the grazing lands, on which stock were fattened, and the families of Adams and Ireland farmed the greater part of the land for several generations, so that their history is inseparably connected with that of the village. In the year 1790 Mr. Francis Ireland bought an estate at the back of the " Abbey Arms " called Rose Gardens. The house was a very old one. The best rooms were all wainscoted in carved oak, surrounded by large walnut trees of great value. He had only one son (James), and in 1799, this son being about to marry, he purchased Loft House, a much larger estate in New Barn Street, with a house and large garden noted for its orchard, stocked with fruit trees of the choicest kinds, including a very ancient mulberry tree. The house was surrounded by meadow lands, in which he used to graze cattle of all kinds. In those days there were nothing but fields between the house and the River Thames. With the aid of a telescope one could read the names of the vessels on the river. I mention on p. 27 that the eminent Dr. Raffles, of Liverpool, preached as a student in the open air on the step of a house in Richmond Street. Mrs. Adams and Miss Ireland tell me that this is quite true. The father of Dr. Raffles, a solicitor living in Church Street, Spitalfields, was a friend of their father's, and used often to drive out on Sunday for a breath of country air, dine at Mr. Ireland's, and go in the evening to hear his son preach. Mr. James Ireland died in 1828, and his father, with his four grandsons, kept up the farm. Mr. Adams came to live in Plaistow a few years before Mr. Francis Ireland. They employed between them large numbers of labourers, both men and women. Mr. Francis Ireland died in 1833 in his 93rd year, and Mrs. James Ireland died in 1876 in her 100th year. The old homestead, Loft House, was sold at her death. The orchard and garden are now a ploughed field, and the meadows are covered with cottages. In 1844 Mr. William Ireland (son of James) lived in the old house which stood almost on the site of the Wesleyan Chapel in High Street. This was once occupied by a rich citizen of London named Foot. He was Lord Mayor of London, and his monument will be found in West Ham Church. In Green Gate Street lived a rather celebrated character, Mr. Blood, a descendant of the Colonel Thomas Blood who attempted in 1671 to steal the Crown jewels. He was a steel engraver by profession, a great sportsman and a crack shot. An old engraving is extant showing him riding on a pony, with his gun under his arm and some dogs following. His wife was a very amiable lady, and a strict Dissenter. Mr. Hudson, who is mentioned on p. 55, was, as Mrs. Adams and Miss Ireland inform me, a butcher in Bond Street, who supplied royalty and the aristocracy with meat. He used the marsh land round Cumberland House for fattening cattle for sale in his shop. Every Spring he would journey into Devonshire and buy cattle, which were driven all the way by road to Cumberland House. Mr. Hudson had among his customers the Prince of Wales, afterwards George IV, who was always in debt, and sometimes owed him £1,000. Mrs. Adams and Miss Ireland well remember a bull being kept by Tom Cobley, landlord of the "Abbey Arms," and used for driving a cart, and even for taking people into town. They have heard that the original name of the "Abbey Arms" was the "The Old Crown."

About the year 1780 Mrs. Adams, a widow lady, came to reside in Plaistow. She first lived in what is now called Brunstock Cottage. It was then a very large old-fashioned house, mostly built of wood, with a summer-house like an observatory such as most of the large houses in the village had in those days. Mrs. Adams carried on the business of a farmer. She had four sons, two of whom assisted her. One of her sons, a wine merchant at Reading, died a wealthy man. In the year 1797 Mr. James Adams bought the estate of Bemeside, married, and had a family of eleven children, six sons and five daughters. One son, Mr. John Adams, became a very eminent surgeon, being head of his department at the London Hospital. Strange to say, there is no direct descendant of the family left in Plaistow at the present time. Some died, others left the parish.

J. CURWEN & SONS, MUSIC PRINTERS, PLAISTOW, LONDON, E.

Lightning Source UK Ltd.
Milton Keynes UK
UKOW06f2002050813

214918UK00012B/1206/P